Tar Heels

Tar Heels

How North Carolinians Got Their Nickname

Michael W. Taylor

Raleigh
Division of Archives and History
North Carolina Department of Cultural Resources

North Carolina Department of Cultural Resources
Betty Ray McCain, *Secretary*
Elizabeth F. Buford, *Deputy Secretary*

Division of Archives and History
Jeffrey J. Crow, *Director*
Larry G. Misenheimer, *Deputy Director*

FOREWORD

One of the most frequently asked questions about North Carolina is how did its residents become known as "Tar Heels." Visitors and natives alike often inquire: How old is the nickname? From where did it derive? Why is North Carolina known as both the "Tar Heel State" and the "Old North State?" Now in *Tar Heels: How North Carolinians Got Their Nickname*, Michael W. Taylor explains the origins of the nickname and how and when it gained general acceptance as a term referring to North Carolinians.

Dr. Taylor is an attorney in private practice in Albemarle, North Carolina. He holds B.A. and J.D. degrees from the University of North Carolina at Chapel Hill and M.A. and Ph.D. degrees from Harvard University. He served as a field historian on the staff of Commander Naval Forces Vietnam during the Vietnam War. He lives near New London, North Carolina, with his wife and three sons and is the author of three books: *The Tyrant Slayers: The Heroic Image in 5th. Century B.C. Athenian Politics and Art* (New York: Arno Press, 1981; Salem, N.H.: Ayer Company Publishers, 1991); *The Cry is War, War, War: The Civil War Correspondence of Lieutenants George Job Huntley and Burwell Thomas Cotton, 34th. Regiment North Carolina Troops* (Dayton, Oh.: Morningside House, 1994); and *To Drive the Enemy from Southern Soil: The Letters of Colonel Francis Marion Parker and the History of the 30th. Regiment North Carolina Troops* (Dayton, Oh.: Morningside House, 1998).

Joe A. Mobley, *Administrator*
Historical Publications Section

October 1999

ACKNOWLEDGMENTS

Many people have helped me in my search for the origin of the nickname "Tar Heel." First and foremost, I must thank William S. Powell, professor emeritus at the University of North Carolina at Chapel Hill and chairman of the North Carolina Historical Commission, for his original research and writing on the subject and his encouragement of my research over the past several years. Professor Powell also was kind enough to read a draft of this publication. Author and Civil War historian Greg Mast, of Roxboro, obtained the William B. A. Lowrance Diary (which contained the earliest written use yet found of the nickname "Tar Heel," in February 1863), brought it to my attention, and gave it to the North Carolina State Archives. Mr. Mast also suggested to me the ultimate conclusion of this booklet that "Tar Heel" originally meant a North Carolina Confederate soldier. Robert Krick, chief historian, Fredericksburg and Spotsylvania National Military Park, has provided me with all instances of the term "Tar Heel" that he has encountered. John Bass of Spring Hope, North Carolina, was always willing to share his knowledge of North Carolina Civil War history and Confederate imprints. Down through the years, William S. Price Jr., David Olson, and George Stevenson of the North Carolina Division of Archives and History have been unfailingly helpful to a lawyer trying to write North Carolina Civil War history on the side. I also wish to thank James O. Sorrell, archivist with the State Archives, for his assistance. The personnel of the Stanly County Public Library Reference Department, including Lu Koontz, Erin Allen, and Jonathan Harwood, have been very helpful for years in obtaining interlibrary loans and other reference materials. Jim Harward and Robert Mabry in Albemarle, North Carolina, are continually sharing their knowledge with me. I am grateful to Joe Mobley and his staff in the Historical Publications Section for their efforts in seeing my manuscript into print. Finally, I must thank my wife, Susan, and our three sons, William, Samuel, and John, for being supportive of my interest in the role of our State in 1861-1865 and in how we came to be called "Tar Heels."

Michael W. Taylor

October 1999

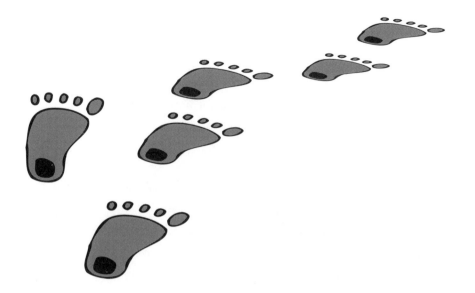

North Carolina's nickname, the "Tar Heel State," probably has a more obscure origin and has inspired more debate as to its meaning than any other nickname among the states of the United States of America. In fact, the nickname "Tar Heel" is a testimony to the humble yet proud origins of the people of North Carolina and to their fiercely independent character.

According to the *Oxford English Dictionary*, "Tar Heel" is the nickname for a native or resident of North Carolina. Many natives and persons who become residents of North Carolina have often wondered about the origin of such an unusual nickname. One obvious explanation is the large number of pine trees that abound in North Carolina. The production and export of tar, pitch, and turpentine, which are derived from pine trees, were for many decades North Carolina's economic mainstays. In the colonial period, for instance, North Carolina was renowned as a source of naval stores, including pine tar so necessary for caulking the hulls of wooden ships. William Gordon, an Anglican missionary from England, found tar to be a major commodity of North Carolina in his inspection tour in 1709. From 1720 to 1870, North Carolina led the world in the production of naval stores. In the eighteenth century, North Carolina produced seven-tenths of the tar, more than half the turpentine, and one-fifth of the pitch exported to England from the colonies.

For many decades, tar and other naval stores (pitch and turpentine) were the chief economic commodities for North Carolina. The state's many pine trees produced the resinous juices harvested for the manufacturing of those products. The above and following two engravings depict the steps in gathering, processing, and distributing naval stores. Courtesy of the State Archives, Division of Archives and History, Raleigh.

William Gaston.

Despite, however, North Carolina's connection to tar, pitch, and turpentine, thus far the term "Tar Heel" has not been found to exist before the Civil War. Prior to that time, North Carolina was called the "Old North State." The state song, "The Old North State," was written by Justice William Gaston in 1840 and adopted as the state song by the General Assembly in 1927. It sings the praises of North Carolina with the refrain: "Hurrah! Hurrah! The Old North State forever." Even during the Civil War, the "Old North State" was

THE OLD NORTH STATE

(Traditional air as sung in 1926)

WILLIAM GASTON

Collected and arranged
by MRS. E. E. RANDOLPH

North Carolina is also known as "The Old North State," a name derived from the state song, "The Old North State," written by Justice William Gaston in 1840. "The Old North State" (above) from *the Old North State Fact Book* (Raleigh: Division of Archives and History, Department of Cultural Resources, 1997), 55. Engraving of Gaston (adjacent page) courtesy of State Archives.

probably the most commonly used nickname for North Carolina in the North and South. Both Civil War presidents, Abraham Lincoln and Jefferson Davis, referred to North Carolina as the "Old North State." Ships in the Confederate and Union navies were named the "North State."

One of the best indications that the term "Tar Heel" was unknown prior to the Civil War is the fact that the nickname was not officially applied to any of North Carolina's military units or to any ship during that conflict. After the Civil War broke out, North Carolina, as part of the newly created Confederacy, recruited companies containing 110 men each, the basic military unit of the time, in every county of the state. Almost every North Carolina company formed for Confederate service adopted a colorful nickname: the "Dry Pond Dixies" of Lincoln County in Company C, 52nd. Regiment North Carolina Troops; the "Ashpole True Boys" of Robeson County in Company F, 51st. Regiment North Carolina Troops; the "Stanly Yankee Hunters" of Stanly County in Company D, 28th. Regiment North Carolina Troops; the "Pee Dee Wildcats" of Anson County in Company K, 26th. Regiment North Carolina Troops; and the "Sons of Mars" of Richmond County in Company D, 46th. Regiment North Carolina Troops. However, not a single company adopted the term "Tar Heel" as part of its nickname. Had the label "Tar Heel" been in common use at the time of the Civil War, undoubtedly it would have been adopted by at least one of the many North Carolina military companies.

Nevertheless, the origin of the term "Tar Heel" probably can be traced to the Civil War. Circumstantial evidence indicates that the nickname was originally coined in the early days of the war as a derogatory label for North Carolina soldiers in the Army of Northern Virginia by soldiers of other Southern states, particularly Virginia. When the lank and lean denizens of the North Carolina piney woods began to pour into Virginia in 1861 as soldiers in the Confederate army, their crude and humble appearance inspired some waggish Virginia soldiers to call them "Tar Heels," a practice that continued and grew as the war progressed. At the Second Battle of Fredericksburg in May 1863, Virginia troops shouted out to a passing North Carolina brigade: "Now Tar Heels when you get out yonder clap your foot down and stick." But the earliest *written* use of the term "Tar Heel" that has yet been found is in a diary entry made on February 6, 1863, by Second Lieutenant William B. A. Lowrance of the 46th. Regiment North Carolina Troops, while encamped in Pender or Onslow County, North Carolina. "I know now," wrote Lowrance, "what is meant by the piney woods region of North Carolina and the idea occurs to me that it is no wonder we are called 'Tar Heels.'"

North Carolina soldiers at first resented the implications that they were second-class fighting men deserving of a demeaning nickname. They insisted that they had joined the Confederate cause for the same patriotic and honorable reasons as their Virginia counterparts, and they maintained that they were equally courageous on the battlefield. In late May 1862, several hundred men of the 28th. Regiment North Carolina Troops were taken prisoner at Hanover Courthouse, Virginia. Just after the battle, a Northern reporter, George Alfred Townsend of the *New York Herald*, mingled with the "brown, brawny, and wiry captives" and recorded the statements of the privates as to why they had enlisted:

> One person said that he enlisted for the honor of his family that "fit in the American Revolution," and another came out to "hev a squint et the fightin." Several were northern and foreign lads that were working on Carolina railroads and could not leave the section, and some labored under the impression that they were to have a "slice" of land and a slave, in the event of Southern independence. A few comprehended the spirit of the contest and took arms from principle; a few also declared their enemity to "Yankee institutions," and seized the occasion to "polish them off," and " give them a ropein' in," but said it was "dull in our deestreeks, an' the slaves was runnin' away so I thought I'ud jine the foces."

When Townsend approached the officers clustered to one side in the prisoners' pen he heard one North Carolina officer complain of the unjustified criticism leveled at North Carolinians by Virginians:

> We have lost mo' men, he said, than any otha'
> Commonwealth; but the Vuhginians, whose soil by ____! Suh,
> we defend suh! Yes suh! Whose soil we defend; these

The earliest *written* use of the term "Tar Heel" that has yet been found is in a diary entry, February 6, 1863, by Second Lieutenant William B. A. Lowrance, who wrote: "I know now what is meant by the piney woods region of North Carolina and the idea occurs to me that it is no wonder we are called 'Tar Heels.'" Excerpt from Lowrance's diary courtesy of State Archives.

Vuhginians, stigmatize us as cowads! *We,* suh! Yes suh, *we,* that nevah wanted to leave the Union,—*we cowads*! Look at ou' blood, suh, ou' blood! That's it, by ____! Look at that! shed on every field of the old Dominion,—killed, muhded, captured, crippled! We *cowads*! I want you [to] prent that!

Throughout the war, Virginians continued to demean North Carolina troops by referring to them as "Tar Heels." During the Shenandoah Valley campaign of 1864, George Quintus Pettus, a soldier in the 13th. Virginia Infantry, in his diary depicted "Tar Heels" as little more than wild men who had wandered up to Virginia from the primeval forest. On one occasion in the valley, he "Was very much surprised to hear . . . people here saying 'Youens' [and] 'We-ens' like the Tarheels." Later he observed that "At one resting place, two Tar Heels got into a fight and one struck the other on the head with a musket and when we passed he was still insensible with the blood running out of his head." Upon purchasing a cup of Shenandoah apple butter, Pettus noted, "The Tarheels call this 'red spread.'" In August, Pettus recorded that the "Tar Heels" sent out a detail to forage for roasting ears of corn. "I don't supposed they paid for them," he remarked tartly. Pettus even blamed North Carolinians for the Confederate rout at Fisher's Hill, Virginia, in September 1864: "The Tarheels gave way first. Their officers cursed and beat them with their swords and tried hard to make them stand, but they could not." Actually, Pettus's claim was unjust. The Virginia cavalry commanded by Brig. Gen. Lunsford L. Lomax had in fact been the first to collapse under a Union flank attack.

Even within the borders of their own state, North Carolinians suffered the insult of being called "Tar Heels" by natives of other Confederate states. Confederate naval lieutenant R. H. Bacot, a South Carolinian who commanded the *CSS Neuse* at Kinston, North Carolina, wrote to his sister in March 1864:

> . . . finally to complete our misery we have a crew of long, lank *"Tar Heels"* (N.C.s from the "Piney Woods"). . . . We have one or two good men for a "Neucleus" but I'm afraid the others can never learn anything about a gunboat. You ou[gh]t to see them in boats! It is ridiculous. They are all legs & arms

& while working at the guns their legs get "Tangled" in the tackles & they are always in the wrong place & in each other's way.

From the early days of the Civil War, North Carolinians resented the insults leveled at them by other Confederates. Not only did they object to the derogatory reference to them as "Tar Heels," but they also felt slighted by the Confederate War Department's failure to give promotions and command of brigades to army officers from the Old North State. And no one was more annoyed by the uncomplimentary references to "Tar Heels" and the scarce number of North Carolinians holding important commands in the Confederate army, than their governor, Zebulon Baird Vance. In November 1862 Vance complained in a report on the war to the North Carolina General Assembly about the lack of promotions of North Carolina officers to vacant brigadierships: "It is mortifying to find entire brigades of North Carolina soldiers in the field commanded by strangers, and in many cases our own brave and war-worn colonels are made to give place to colonels from distant States, who are promoted to the command of North Carolina troops over their heads to vacant brigadierships." Vance's annoyance over the credit denied North Carolinians for their war effort reached the level of heated correspondence among him, Secretary of War James A. Seddon, and Gen. Robert E. Lee in the summer of 1863. On July 3, 1863, the very day in which so many North Carolinians fell at the famed but disastrous Pickett-Pettigrew-Trimble charge at Gettysburg, Pennsylvania, Vance wrote Seddon requesting that a North Carolina newspaper correspondent be assigned to Lee's Army of Northern Virginia to record the success and gallantry of North Carolina's sons on the battlefield. "There has been much complaint," the governor declared, "among our people that the participation of our troops in the various battles, has not been noticed, with that commendation to which they are supposed by us to be entitled." Vance therefore insisted that, given the bias of the War Department and the Virginia press, a North Carolina correspondent at Lee's headquarters was necessary "to see that justice was done North Carolina Troops." His complaints were not without basis, for the Richmond newspapers bitterly and unfairly blamed the failure of Pickett-Pettigrew-Trimble charge at Gettysburg on the wavering of North Carolina troops. Three weeks after Gettysburg, on July 26, 1863, upon being advised by Seddon that a special North Carolina correspondent would not be allowed to accompany Lee's army, Vance replied to the secretary of war: "I beg leave to withdraw the request. The troops from N. C. can afford to appeal to history. I am confident that they have but little to expect from their associates."

Indeed, there were many instances to validate the history of the battle-hardened "Tar Heels," who frequently fought with a courage and ferocity that shamed their Virginia counterparts. For instance, according to one eye witness at the Battle of Chancellorsville on May 3, 1863, as a North Carolina brigade charged the enemy, "The brave, chivalric Virginians lay flat on the ground and the 'tar heels' whom they so often ridicule walked over them to glory and to victory." General Lee credited North Carolina troops with saving the day for the Confederates at the Battle of Spotslvania Courthouse, Virginia, in May of 1864. On the twelfth of that month the North Carolina brigade commanded by Brig. Gen. Stephen Dodson Ramseur stemmed the tide of the Federal breakthrough into the so-called Bloody Angle. "The first men that came to our assistance was that brigade of North Carolinians commanded by the peerless Ramseur," recalled one participant in the battle. According to tradition, General Lee himself may have bestowed a positive connotation on the term "Tar Heels." Tradition and newly discovered evidence indicates that following the Confederate success at the Battle of Reams's Station in August 1864, he reportedly cried out, "Thank God for the Tar Heel boys!" That Lee possibly spoke such a phrase is supported to some extent by the testimony of Maj. Joseph Engelhard, adjutant of Maj. Gen. Cadmus M. Wilcox's division. Following the battle at Reams's Station, a major Confederate victory, Engelhard wrote to a friend that "It was a 'Tar Heel' fight," which resulted in "Genl. Lee . . . *thanking God* which you know means something brilliant." Regardless of the exact nature of what Lee might have uttered in regard to the behavior of the "Tar Heels, the general had nothing but the highest praise for their performance in the battle. He wrote to Governor Vance:

> I have frequently been called upon to mention the services of
> North Carolina soldiers in this army, but their gallantry and

Gen. Robert E. Lee himself might have used the term "Tar Heel" following the Confederate success at the Battle of Reams's Station, when he reportedly proclaimed, "Thank God for the Tar Heel boys!" Engraving courtesy of State Archives.

conduct was never more deserving of admiration than in the engagement at Reams' Station. The brigades of Generals [John R.] Cooke, [William] MacRae, and [James H.] Lane, the last under the command of General [James] Conner, advanced through a thick abatis of felled trees, under a heavy fire of musketry and artillery, and carried the enemy's works with a steady courage that elicited the warm commendation of their corps and division commanders and the admiration of the army.

General Lee's praise of "Tar Heels" is verified to some extend by Maj. Joseph Engelhard who wrote following the Battle of Reams's Station: "It was a Tar Heel Fight," which resulted in "Genl Lee . . . *thanking God.*" Excerpt from Engelhard letter courtesy of State Archives.

Although North Carolina troops at first bridled under the insult of "Tar Heels" hurled at them by the soldiers of the Old Dominion and other Confederate states, they soon learned to retaliate by retorting that Confederate soldiers from other states might improve their own battlefield performance if they too had tar on their heels. When Mississippians shouted the hurtful epithet at a limping North Carolina mountaineer immediately after the Second Battle of Fredericksburg in May 1863—when the Confederate lines on Marye's Heights had been broken and later restored—the mountaineer replied: "Yes d___ you. If yer hadder had some tar on yer own heels yestiddy, yer would er stuck to them thar works better, and we wouldn't er had to put yer back thar."

Gradually, North Carolina's soldiers lost their sensitivity to the term "Tar Heels" as a derogatory label. In the early months of 1863, during a review of the corps of Gen. Leonidas Polk at Shelbyville, Tennessee, when someone called out "Hurrah for the Tar Heels," Sgt. William B. Breeden, the regimental ensign (flag bearer) for the 39th. Regiment North Carolina Troops, "took it as an insult, and stepped out of the ranks, stuck his flagstaff up in the ground and dared those offering an insult to North Carolina to step out two at a time and he would whip the entire regiment." Lt. John M. Davidsion of the Thirty-ninth, recalled that "This caused a yell of laughter, and Breedon [sic], realizing the joke, raised his banner and marched on." Davidson noted that Breeden took such heated offense "because we had not yet learned our new name." But eventually, the men of the Old North State embraced their new nickname with pride. A soldier's letter published in the Raleigh *Daily Progress* on July 28, 1863, describing the Battle of Gettysburg was signed "Tar Heel."

None other than North Carolina governor Zebulon Baird Vance planted the final official seal of approval on the nickname of "Tar Heels" for his state's Confederate soldiers. The occasion of Vance's endorsement came when he visited the Army of Northern Virginia and delivered a speech to North Carolina troops on March 28, 1864. Pvt. Walter R. Battle of the 4th. Regiment North Carolina Troops described the governor's remarks: " He [Vance] said it did not sound right to address us as 'Fellow Soldiers,' because he was not one of us—he used to be until he shirked out of the service for a little office

Gov. Zebulon Baird Vance bestowed the official approval of the nickname "Tar Heels" when he delivered a speech to North Carolina troops on March 28, 1864. According to one of the soldiers, the governor addressed them "as 'fellow Tar Heels,' as we always stick." Photograph of Vance courtesy of Mrs. Graham A. Barden, New Bern. Copy by State Archives.

down in North Carolina, so now he would address us as 'Fellow Tar Heels,' as we always stick."

By the final days of the Civil War, the nickname "Tar Heels" had gained wide acceptance among North Carolinians to describe themselves proudly and affectionately. In a letter written near

Petersburg, Virginia, on December 31, 1864, North Carolina brigadier general James H. Lane declared:

> Governor Vance now has a large quantity of sorghum lying at Greensboro awaiting Transportation. He says he is willing to send his "tar heels" a great many things to help along, if they will only furnish him with the requisite transportation. I really believe the North Carolina soldiers fare better than any others in the army, as much as some ignorant people are disposed to laugh at the "Old North State."

Following the Civil War, the use of the term "Tar Heel" became widespread in North Carolina, and ultimately the phrase "Tar Heel State" assumed a place alongside the older "Old North State." Today, North Carolinians recognize and honor their state by both titles. The more colorful term "Tar Heel State," however, probably has become the more familiar of the two.

The first known published post-Civil War reference to "Tar Heel" was the sheet music printed in Baltimore in 1866 by William C. Miller titled "Wearin' of the Grey written by Tar Heel." The first town in North Carolina certain to have been named Tar Heel was the community of that name founded in 1875 (incorporated 1963) in Bladen County. One tradition holds that the town's name was given to the site by the troops of British general Cornwallis during the American Revolution, who allegedly emerged from the nearby Cape Fear River with tar on their heels. Tar and other naval stores were, of course, produced in the vicinity, and legend says that the "ground was covered with tar, and so were the feet that passed over it." But it is most unlikely that the name of the site had been designated "Tar Heel" prior to the Civil War. In all probability, the community acquired its name as a result of the term originating and gaining acceptance during the Civil War.

Over the years, the term "Tar Heel" has become a widely accepted and frequently seen label for individuals and institutions. It is a standard nickname for anyone from North Carolina. About 1926, the football team at the University of North Carolina at Chapel Hill changed its name from the "White Phantoms" to the "Tar Heels." All the sports teams from that school now have that nickname.

The correct spelling for the name is two capitalized words—
"Tar Heel"—although the one-word "Tarheel" is often seen,
especially in the names of businesses. A 1999 check of the Internet
revealed 294 listings of businesses named "Tarheel" in 229
categories and 149 listings of businesses named "Tar Heel" in 116
categories, with building contractors and used car dealers being the
most common.

By the end of the Civil War, North Carolina's soldiers described themselves proudly
and affectionately as "Tar Heels." On December 31, 1864, the state's Brig. Gen.
James H. Lane noted that Governor Vance always ensured that "his 'Tar Heels'"
were well supplied. Photograph of portrait of Lane courtesy of State Archives.

The first known published post-Civil War reference to "Tar Heel" was the sheet music "Wearin' of the Grey written by Tar Heel," printed in 1866. A copy of the music appears on this and the following three pages. Courtesy of State Archives.

WEARIN' OF THE GREY.

Written by Tar Heel.

1. Oh! John-ny dear, and did you hear, the news that's late-ly spread, That
2. *Then since the co - lor we must wear is of the hate-ful blue, The*

nev - er - more the South-ern cross must rear its state - ly head; The
chil - dren of the Sun - ny South must be to mem'- ry true; Ah!

"White and Reds'," for-bid by law, so Northmen proud-ly say, Nor
take the cock-ade from their hats and tread it 'neath the feet, *And*

you, nor I, can e'er a-gain be "Wear-in' of the Grey!" And
still tho' bruis'd and mangled sad, 'twill speak a lan-guage sweet: *And*

when we meet with strangers kind, who take us by the hand, En-
bu-ried in our heart of hearts the precious words lie hid, *Where*

-quir-ing warm-ly of the South, our own be-lov-ed land,
oft they call the bit-ter tears to wet the droop-ing lid,

We've bound to tell the wo-ful truth, let cost what-e'er it may, *That*
But let them flow they do us good thro' all the mournful day, *While*

Repeat as Chorus.

some are threat-en'd e'en with death, for "Wear-in' of the Grey!"
con-stant we do call to mind the "Wear-in' of the Grey!"

3.

And if at last our fathers' law be torn from Southland's heart,
Her sons will take their household gods and far away depart;
Rememb'ring still the whisper'd word, to weary wand'rers giv'n,
That justice pure, and perfect rest, are found alone in heav'n.
Then on some green and distant isle beneath the setting sun,
We'll patient wait the coming time when life and earth are done,
Nor even in the dying hour while passing calm away,
Can we forget or e'er regret the "Wearin' of the Grey!"

SOURCES

Andrews, J. Cutler. *The North Reports the Civil War*. Pittsburg: University of Pittsburg Press, 1958.

Botkin, B. A., ed. *A Treasury of Southern Folklore*. New York: Crown Publishers, 1949.

Clark, Walter, ed. *Histories of the Several Regiments and Battalions from North Carolina in the Great War, 1861-'65*. 5 vols. Raleigh: State of North Carolina, 1901.

Cummings, C. C. "Chancellorsville, May 2, 1863," *Confederate Veteran* 23 (September 1915): 405.

Daily Progress (Raleigh), 1863.

George Quintus Pettus Diary Transcript. Records of National Military Park, Fredericksburg, Virginia.

Johnson, Hugh Buckner, ed. "The Civil War Letters of George Boardman Battle and Walter Raleigh Battle of Wilson, North Carolina." Typescript in Wilson County Public Library, Wilson, North Carolina.

Johnston, Frontis W. and Joe A. Mobley, eds. *The Papers of Zebulon Baird Vance*. 2 vols. to date. Raleigh: Division of Archives and History, Department of Cultural Resources, 1963—.

Jones, John B. *A Rebel War Clerk's Diary at the Confederate State Capital*. 2 vols. Philadelphia: J. B. Lippincott, 1866.

Joseph Engelhard to "Friend Ruf," August 28,1864. Tar Heel Collection. Private Collections. State Archives, Division of Archives and History, Raleigh.

Journal of William McWillie. State Archives, Mississippi Department of Archives and History, Jackson, Mississippi.

Manarin, Louis H. and Weymouth T. Jordan, comps. *North Carolina Troops, 1861-1865: A Roster*. 14 vols. to date. Raleigh: Division of Archives and History, Department of Cultural Resources, 1963—.

The Old North State Fact Book. Raleigh: Division of Archives and History, Department of Cultural Resources, 1997.

Oxford English Dictionary.

Powell, William S. *The North Carolina Gazetteer*. Chapel Hill: University of North Carolina Press, 1968.

——————————. "What's in a Name?" *Tar Heel* (March 1982).

R. H. Bacot Letters, 1864-1865. Private Collections. State Archives, Division of Archives and History, Raleigh.

Saunders, William L., ed. *The Colonial Records of North Carolina*. 10 vols. Raleigh: State of North Carolina, 1886-1890.

Taylor, Michael W. *To Drive the Enemy from Southern Soil: The Letters of Colonel Francis Marion Parker and the History of the 30th. Regiment N.C.T.* Dayton, Oh.: Morningside Bookshop, 1998.

——————————. "North Carolina in the Pickett-Pettigrew-Trimble Charge at Gettysburg," *Gettysburg Magazine* 8 (January 1993): 67-93.

Townsend, George Alfred. *Campaigns of a Non-Combatant*. New York: Blelock and Company, 1866.

The War of the Rebellion: A Compilation of the Official Records of the Union and Confederate *Armies*. 70 vols. Washington: Government Printing Office, 1888-1901.

"Wearin' of the Grey, Written by Tar Heel: Arranged for the Piano Forte." Baltimore: William C. Miller, 1866. Copy in Tar Heel Collection. Private Collections. State Archives, Division of Archives and History, Raleigh.

William B. A. Lowrance Diary. Tar Heel Collection. Private Collections. State Archives, Division of Archives and History, Raleigh.

William Calder Papers. Southern Historical Collection. University of North Carolina Library at Chapel Hill.